HIT SONGS FOR TWO

T0083983

Arrangements by Peter Deneff

ISBN 978-1-5400-1280-7

7777 W. BLUEMOUND RD. P.O. BOX 13819 MILWAUKEE, WI 53213

Visit Hal Leonard Online at
www.halleonard.com

CONTENTS

4   All About That Bass

6   All of Me

8   Brave

10   Budapest

12   Can't Stop the Feeling

14   Grenade

16   Hey, Soul Sister

18   Home

20   I Will Wait

22   Let Her Go

24   Let It Go

26   100 Years

28   Poker Face

30   Royals

32   Say Something

34   Shake It Off

36   Shape of You

38   Skyfall

40   Some Nights

42   Stay with Me

44   Story of My Life

46   Viva La Vida

ALL ABOUT THAT BASS

TROMBONES

Words and Music by KEVIN KADISH
and MEGHAN TRAINOR

ALL OF ME

TROMBONES

Words and Music by JOHN STEPHENS
and TOBY GAD

8

BRAVE

TROMBONES

Words and Music by SARA BAREILLES
and JACK ANTONOFF

BUDAPEST

TROMBONES

Words and Music by GEORGE BARNETT
and JOEL POTT

CAN'T STOP THE FEELING
from TROLLS

TROMBONES

Words and Music by JUSTIN TIMBERLAKE,
MAX MARTIN and SHELLBACK

GRENADE

TROMBONES

Words and Music by BRUNO MARS,
ARI LEVINE, PHILIP LAWRENCE,
BRODY BROWN, CLAUDE KELLY
and ANDREW WYATT

Moderately

HEY, SOUL SISTER

TROMBONES

Words and Music by PAT MONAHAN,
ESPEN LIND and AMUND BJORKLUND

HOME

TROMBONES

Words and Music by GREG HOLDEN
and DREW PEARSON

I WILL WAIT

TROMBONES

Words and Music by
MUMFORD & SONS

Moderately

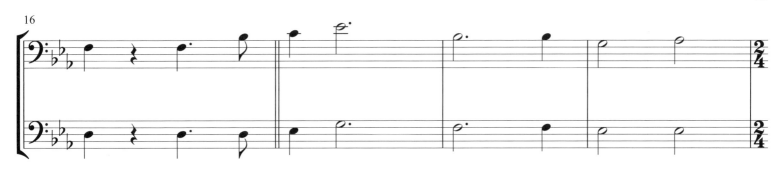

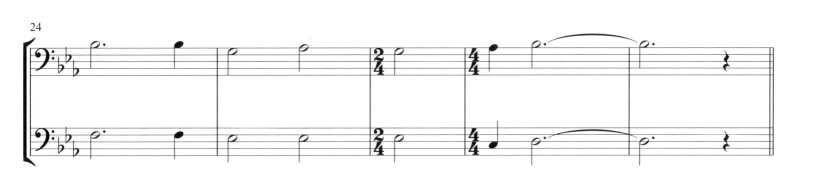

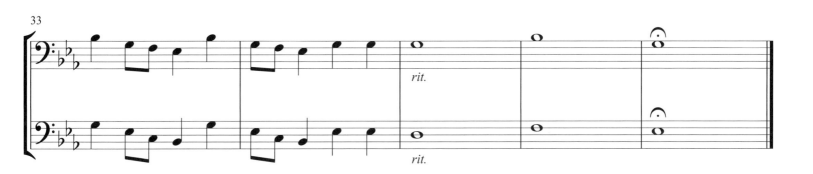

LET HER GO

TROMBONES

Words and Music by
MICHAEL DAVID ROSENBERG

LET IT GO

TROMBONES

Words and Music by JAMES BAY
and PAUL BARRY

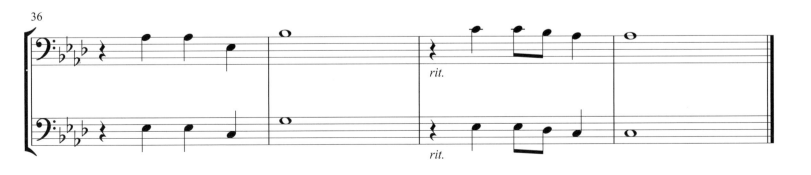

100 YEARS

TROMBONES

Words and Music by
JOHN ONDRASIK

POKER FACE

TROMBONES

Words and Music by STEFANI GERMANOTTA
and RedOne

ROYALS

TROMBONES

Words and Music by ELLA YELICH-O'CONNOR
and JOEL LITTLE

Moderately

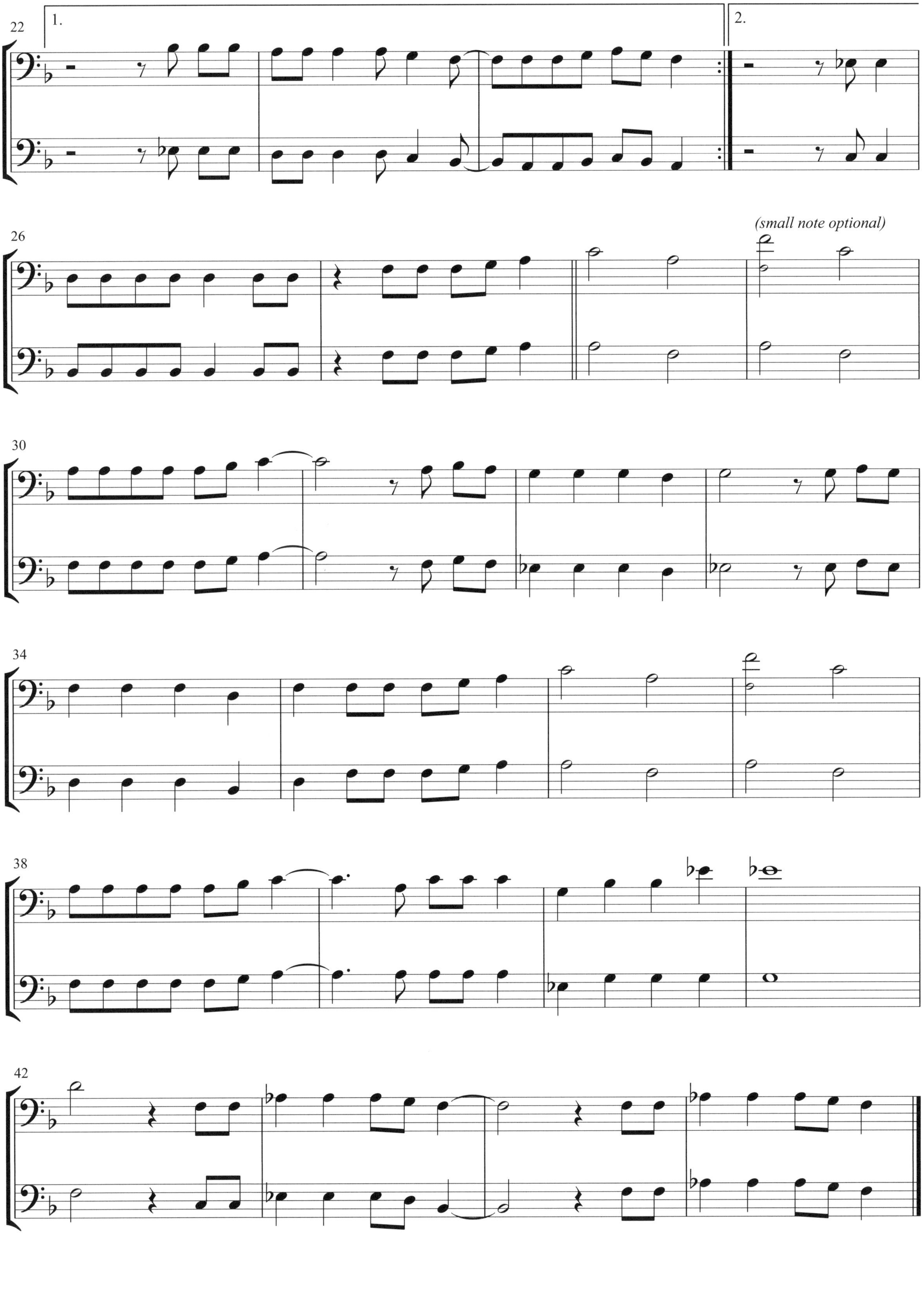
22
1.
2.
26
(small note optional)
30
34
38
42

SAY SOMETHING

TROMBONES

Words and Music by IAN AXEL,
CHAD VACCARINO and MIKE CAMPBELL

SHAKE IT OFF

TROMBONES

Words and Music by TAYLOR SWIFT,
MAX MARTIN and SHELLBACK

SHAPE OF YOU

TROMBONES

Words and Music by ED SHEERAN,
KEVIN BRIGGS, KANDI BURRUSS,
TAMEKA COTTLE, STEVE MAC
and JOHNNY McDAID

Moderately fast

SKYFALL
from the Motion Picture SKYFALL

TROMBONES

Words and Music by ADELE ADKINS
and PAUL EPWORTH

SOME NIGHTS

TROMBONES

Words and Music by JEFF BHASKER,
ANDREW DOST, JACK ANTONOFF
and NATE RUESS

STAY WITH ME

TROMBONES

Words and Music by SAM SMITH,
JAMES NAPIER, WILLIAM EDWARD PHILLIPS,
TOM PETTY and JEFF LYNNE

STORY OF MY LIFE

TROMBONES

Words and Music by JAMIE SCOTT,
JOHN HENRY RYAN, JULIAN BUNETTA,
HARRY STYLES, LIAM PAYNE, LOUIS TOMLINSON,
NIALL HORAN and ZAIN MALIK

VIVA LA VIDA

TROMBONES

Words and Music by GUY BERRYMAN,
JON BUCKLAND, WILL CHAMPION
and CHRIS MARTIN

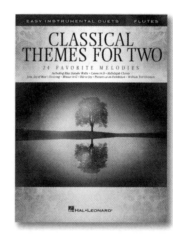